Substances for use at work: the provision of information

Health and Safety series booklet HS(G)27 (rev)

Contents

London: Her Majesty's Stationery Office

HS(G) series
The purpose of this series is to provide guidance for those who have duties under the Health and Safety at Work etc Act 1974 and other relevant legislation. It gives guidance on the practical application of legislation, but it should not be regarded as an authoritative interpretation of the law.

Enquiries regarding this or any other HSE publications should be addressed to the HSE Information Centres at the following addresses:

Broad Lane
SHEFFIELD
S3 7HQ
Telephone: (0742) 752539
Fax: (0742) 720006

Baynards House
1 Chepstow Place
Westbourne Grove
LONDON
W2 4TF
Telephone: (071) 221 0870
Fax: (071) 221 9178

ISBN 0 11 885458 5

Introduction

Although many substances may present hazards they can still be used without risks to health and safety provided these hazards are understood and the appropriate precautions are taken. The key to this is the preparation of adequate information about the substance and the risks in the reasonably foreseeable uses followed by effective communication of the information through the chain of supply.

Legal framework

The legal basis for the provision of information on substances is contained primarily in the HSW Act 1974, Sections 2 and 6. Section 6, as amended by the Consumer Protection Act 1987, places general duties upon manufacturers, importers and suppliers of substances. They must take such steps as are necessary to provide adequate information about any risks to health or safety to which the inherent properties of the substance may give rise, about the results of any relevant tests on the substance and about any conditions necessary to ensure that the substance will be safe and without risk to health when it is being used, handled, processed, stored, transported or disposed of by a person at work or in premises to which Section 4 of the HSW Act applies. For the purposes of this guidance, where the context requires, the word 'use' will include handling, processing, storing, transporting and disposing of.

Section 2 requires an employer to ensure the health and safety of all his employees. Employees need to be kept properly informed and the general duties to this effect under Section 2 are reinforced by the Safety Representatives and Safety Committees Regulations 1977 and the associated Code of Practice. Additional requirements with respect to the protection of persons other than employees, for example, members of the public, are covered by Section 3 of the HSW Act.

The extension of the duty under Section 6 to include Section 4, places duties on persons who control premises which are non-domestic and used as a place of work or a place where people use plant or substances. The intention is to provide protection for persons at work on those premises and persons not at work who are on the premises. Examples of section 4 premises would be garages where members of the public come and use equipment to maintain their cars or a launderette where people use washing machines and powders.

This guidance outlines these duties and suggests how they should be interpreted in a practical way. The HSC will continue to examine the provision of information on substances as European Directives in this field emerge. The Control of Substances Hazardous to Health (COSHH) Regulations 1988 also have a bearing on this guidance, particularly Part 3. Employers need adequate information about the substances they use if they are to make an adequate assessment of risks to health.

Use of the guidance

To allow the reader to refer quickly to the relevant sections the guidance is divided into three main parts, subsections of which are listed in the Contents.

Part 1 outlines the general principles and, in particular, explains why the user of a substance needs to know about the hazards and about any precautions that should be taken. This sets the framework by which manufacturers, importers and suppliers of substances should interpret their duty to prepare and provide adequate information. Emphasis is placed on a flexible and inquiring approach to meet the needs of the particular situation or market.

Part 2 gives guidance to manufacturers, importers and suppliers on the general content of this information package. The duty to carry out research and testing is outlined and emphasis is placed on careful evaluation of the results in the light of the reasonably foreseeable uses of the substance. Although a standardised information sheet format is not proposed a simple check list is suggested to ensure that there are no fundamental omissions in the information package. Each main item in this check list is explained and some illustrations are given of typical approaches.

Part 3 concentrates on the role of the employer who needs to secure a safe working environment for all his employees and others who may be affected by the work activities. Advice is also given for persons with duties under Section 4. The information provided by the manufacturer should be interpreted carefully and should be assessed so that suitable safe plant and safe working procedures can be devised and employees are properly protected. In many circumstances the employer will need to consult in detail with suppliers, employees and possibly other parties to ensure that comprehensive information and advice is being received and acted upon.

Part 1 General principles

The user's need to know

1 The scope of Section 6 has been widened by the amendment under the Consumer Protection Act to cover all substances. Section 6 now covers all substances when being handled etc. at work or in situations to which Section 4 applies. The hazards of substances for use at work* vary widely. Most risks can be controlled if the hazards are understood and the appropriate precautions taken. The hazards of most immediate concern may be those of fire and explosion or of sudden gassing or poisoning and more direct dangers, such as slipping on spillages or drowning. However, other hazards such as long term effects on health or dangerous reactions with other substances are equally important. Manufacturers must ensure as the first part of their duty that so far as is reasonably practicable† the substances they supply will be safe and without risk to health when properly used. They can do this by using relevant existing research results, or either conducting their own tests or arranging for them to be carried out. When this work is completed the second stage of the duty is to ensure that the users‡ are provided with adequate information about the hazards from the inherent properties of the substance which may give rise to risks to health and safety in use. Appropriate conditions for safe use can then be devised. Many incidents have been caused by failures in the communication of information on hazards.

Duties of employers

2 Employers have a general duty under Section 2 of HSWA concerning the health, safety and welfare at work of all their employees. This duty extends to arrangements for ensuring, so far as is reasonably practicable, safety and absence of risks to health in connection with the use, handling, storage and transport of articles and

*The expression 'substance for use at work' is defined in Section 53 of the HSW Act as: "any natural or artificial substance, whether in solid or liquid form or in the form of a gas or vapour ...... intended for use (whether exclusively or not) by persons at work" and includes micro-organisms. These are defined as any microscopic biological entity which is capable of replication.

Among the common terms used to describe substances are 'materials', 'chemicals', 'mixtures' and 'preparations'. Most substances will not contain a single pure component. Sometimes the impurities may present a greater hazard than the substance. Many will be of complex and variable composition such as paints, adhesives, certain solvents, oils or cleaning fluids. The term 'substance' also covers more conventional materials, such as clay, sand or wood, and less obvious materials, such as toxins produced by plants or animals. The term 'substance' will be used in this wide overall sense throughout the guidance. It should also be recognised that certain articles may present hazards due to the substances they contain (eg asbestos friction materials or lead paint on steel). Section 6 of the HSW Act imposes similar duties for articles as for substances.

†'Reasonably practicable'

In deciding what is reasonably practicable the seriousness of the risk can be weighed against the difficulty and cost of removing or reducing it. In considering the cost no allowance should be made for the size, nature or profitability of the business concerned. Where the difficulty and cost are high, and a careful assessment of the risk shows it to be comparatively unimportant, action may not need to be taken. On the other hand where the risk is high, action must be taken at whatever cost.

‡The term 'use' appears extensively throughout the HSW Act (eg " .... for use .... by persons at work"). It is possible to argue that for practical purposes the user should be construed as being the customer or purchaser of the substance and as such will be an employer or self-employed person with duties under Sections 2 and 3 of the HSW Act or a person with duties under section 4. However, it could be held that 'user' means each individual person involved in a work activity with a substance that has been supplied for this purpose. A common sense approach would suggest that, for the vast majority of purposes, the 'user' will be the employer or customer. However, there may be circumstances when an alternative interpretation would not be unreasonable (see for example paragraph 6).

substances and the provision of any necessary information, instruction, training and supervision to the employees. In addition under Section 3 of HSWA every employer and self-employed person has a duty to persons not in his employment*, but who may be affected thereby, not to expose them to risks to their health and safety so far as is reasonably practicable (Section 2 and 3 are reproduced in Appendix 1).

3 In order to fulfil these duties employer's need reliable information and advice about any substance that are supplied to them. The manufacturer or supplier should provide adequate information. For example, it needs to be interpreted in the light of the special circumstances of use; and it may be necessary to seek further information. This may be needed if the manufacturer is not aware of these circumstances. An employer cannot transfer or abrogate these duties. Section 6 information is thus intended to provide the essential communication link between the manufacturer and the user whether directly or through the supplier or importer.

Duties and information needs of employees

4 Employees who may be at risk of exposure to hazardous substances at their workplace should expect to receive adequate information concerning the nature of the risks and the precautions to take. In particular, an employee needs:

(a) to know about the hazards to which he might be exposed and the likely risk;

(b) to understand the reasons for, and the effectiveness of, safety measures adopted by the employer;

(c) to recognise the symptoms and signs of danger of which he should be aware;

(d) to be able to participate in discussions at shop floor level or as a safety representative or through safety committees.

5 The employer has a duty to provide this guidance through whatever information, instruction, training and supervision is necessary. Additionally, the employer has a duty to consult any trade union appointed safety representative and will also need to provide necessary information to any safety committee (see The Safety Representative and Safety Committees Regulations 1977 (SI No 500) and associated Approved Code of Practice) concerning health and safety matters. In particular, he should make available to them health and safety information about substances used or proposed to be used in the workplace. Safety representatives are empowered to seek such information from the employer and to investigate potential hazards at the workplace.

6 Employees can expect to look to their employer in the first instance for the information they require. This should assist them in carrying out their duties to co-operate with their employer for the purpose of securing compliance with statutory health and safety requirements (Section 7 of the HSW Act). However, there may be legitimate reasons for employees or their safety representatives seeking direct access to manufacturers' or suppliers' literature and advice.

Duties of manufacturers, importers and suppliers

7 Manufacturers, importers and suppliers of substances have a specific duty under Section 6(5) of the HSW Act. They must carry out any necessary research with a view to the discovery and, so far as is reasonably practicable, the elimination or minimisation of any risks to health or safety to which the substances they produce or supply may give rise. Thereafter, manufacturers, importers and suppliers need to comply with the following requirements:

"6(4) *It shall be the duty of any person who manufactures, imports or supplies any substance -*

(a) to ensure, so far as is reasonably practicable, that the substance will be safe

*For example:
- contractors maintaining plant in the workplace
- persons living near the workplace who may be affected by emissions from the workplace or other incidents
- persons using public footpaths to cross agricultural or amenity land which is being or has been sprayed
- emergency services personnel attending incidents at the workplace.

and without risks to health at all times when it is being used, handled, processed, stored or transported by a person at work or in premises to which section 4 above applies;

to carry out or arrange for the carrying out of such testing and examination as may be necessary for the performance of the duty imposed on him by the preceding paragraph;

to take such steps as are necessary to secure that persons supplied by that person with the substance are provided with adequate information about any risks to health or safety to which the inherent properties of the substance may give rise, about the results of any relevant tests which have been carried out on or in connection with the substance and about any conditions necessary to ensure that the substance will be safe and without risks to health at all such times as are mentioned in paragraph (a) above and when the substance is being disposed of; and

(d) to take such steps as are necessary to secure, so far as is reasonably practicable that persons so supplied are provided with all such revisions of information provided to them by virtue of the preceding paragraph as are necessary by reasons of its becoming known that anything gives rise to a serious risk to health or safety ."

The relevant parts of Section 6 are reproduced in Appendix 1. The changes made by the amendment are clearly indicated and compared with the original provisions in Appendix 2.

Sources of information

8 The following sources of information will be relevant in most cases:

(a) information carried on labels complying with the *Classification, Packaging and Labelling of Dangerous Substances Regulations 1984 SI, Control of Pesticides Regulations 1986 (CPLR) SI,*, or from classifying the substances by applying the criteria in those regulations. This information provides a useful guide to the potential hazard, but does not take account of the actual risk likely to arise in all circumstances of use, and so should not be relied upon exclusively (see paragraphs 27 to 31);

(b) guidance material on substances and processes published by the HSE or other authoritative bodies, for example Guidance Note EH40: *Occupational Exposure Limits*; HSE Toxicity Review Series;

(c) experience obtained and information gathered as a result of knowledge of previous use or operating experience with similar substances or processes.

(d) technical reference sources (textbooks, scientific/technical papers, trade journals etc) which may complement information obtained from the manufacturer or supplier or from the other sources;

(e) professional institutions, trade associations, trade unions and other specialist consultancy services.

Searching for information

9 The type of information search that is necessary will depend not only on the inherent properties of the substance, but also on the reasonably foreseeable processing conditions and the arrangements for handling storage and disposal. The user will have detailed knowledge of these and the manufacturer should so far as is reasonably practicable take them into account. For example, if it is intended to react or blend different substances, it will be necessary to investigate properties such as flammability and toxicity both individually and in combination. Similarly if the physical or chemical properties of the substance may be altered in-process (eg by milling to produce a fine dust that could be a health or explosion hazard) then appropriate information will be needed.

10 If the user modifies a substance and then supplies others adequate information must be provided about the changes made which affect risks to health and safety.

The chain of communication

11 The communication chain starts with the

manufacturer, who has the duty under 6(4)(a) to ensure, so far as is reasonably practicable, that the substance will be safe and without risk to health at all times when it is being used either by a person at work or in premises to which Section 4 applies. This will involve carrying out the necessary basic research to evaluate health and safety risks which might arise in using the substance, and to eliminate or minimise these risks, unless this has already been adequately and reliably performed by others. It is then necessary to assemble the information on hazards and precautions into a practical form for the user.

12 The duty to communicate information falls on each person in the supply chain. In some cases the supplier or distributor may re-process or re-package the substance. These changes may require the provision of additional information.

13 The initial onus of responsibility to provide adequate information will be clearly placed on the manufacturer. The amendment to Section 6 has widened the importer's duty to parallel that of domestic manufacturers, except that they do not have to carry out research etc unless they are the manufacturer. The intention is that imported goods should not be subject to any less stringent conditions than domestically produced ones. Thus the onus is on the importer to ensure that adequate health and safety information is provided. The aim is that the user will be able to use the substance without risk to health and safety.

14 A new requirement has been introduced to make sure that information provided to users takes account of advances in knowledge or experience which reveal previously unknown significant hazards. Reasonably practicable steps must be taken to ensure that persons previously supplied with a substance are provided with revised information.

Methods of communication

15 How information should be provided to users will depend on the circumstances. The duty is not a strict requirement to provide full information automatically with every delivery of a substance. For regular customers the provision of a data sheet at yearly or even longer intervals may suffice depending on the type of information, and of course whether there are any amendments to it. Any revision of the information which is necessary because a previously unknown serious risk to health and safety becomes known would need to be done promptly, perhaps by using available customer records. Each person in the supply chain has a duty to provide information. The information must reflect the properties of the substance as supplied and its application.

16 The user may wish to discuss his own particular needs with the supplier in addition to the data which is provided.

The information package

17 The term 'information package' can be used to describe the various means by which a manufacturer, supplier etc imparts information and advice to the user. Key elements of any information package will be:

(a) the product labels;

(b) supplementary general advice such as advisory leaflets and data sheets;

(c) detailed technical advice, when appropriate.

In some cases the information package may stimulate discussions between the user and the supplier to ensure that any particular circumstances are adequately covered.

Adequacy

18 A number of factors affect the adequacy of the information supplied. These include:

(a) the properties of the substance;

(b) the hazards of the substance;

(c) the reasonably foreseeable uses;

(d) the quantity being supplied;

(e) the anticipated knowledge and competence of the user.

19 For example, the routine supply of a known hazardous material to industry in bulk would require a thorough investigation of the potential

hazards and detailed advice to the user. However, a different approach may be required for the supply of a small quantity of a chemical to a specialist laboratory for research purposes.

20 Similarly, a common material such as sand that contains crystalline silica (which may cause lung damage if the dust is fine enough and is inhaled over extended periods) may present different hazards to different industries depending on the grade of sand and the way it is used. Consequently different advice may be appropriate for fine, dry sand supplied to a foundry (where there is a well-known risk of inhaling the fine silica dust) than for a coarser grade of sand used in building works.

21 The manufacturer, supplier etc needs to appraise the information available to him and decide what he needs to provide for the user in particular circumstances. He should always consider the reasonably foreseeable uses but is not expected to deal with bizarre uses.

Sample data sheets

22 Despite the wide variations in format that are possible, certain general principles can be outlined which may help to direct the efforts of those preparing information under Section 6, whether it is for highly hazardous substances or those with little hazard or for any of the variants in between. A model format may have to be supplemented in particular cases.

Part 2 Preparation of an 'information package' by the manufacturer, supplier etc

Research, testing and evaluation of information

23 There is a continuing responsibility under Section 6 of the HSW Act for manufacturers, suppliers and importers to provide information and advice which is accurate and relevant.

24 The type of research and testing that is necessary will depend on several factors including:

(a) the extent of hazard information already available;
(b) the relevance of the existing information to the safe use;
(c) the degree of hazard and the quantities involved.

25 Research, testing and examination need not be repeated by a manufacturer or supplier if it has been carried out elsewhere and the results, published or otherwise, made available. Those making use of such sources of information must satisfy themselves that it is reasonable to rely on the result obtained. In this way manufacturers and suppliers will often be able to relieve themselves of some or all of the burden of actual testing. They should ensure, however, that an adequate 'information package' is compiled from whatever reliable sources are available. This may mean making their own arrangements for research and testing in order to fill any basic information gaps which come to light.

26 It is outside the scope of this guidance booklet to provide detailed advice on the types of test and examination which may be required. However, detailed guidance on testing for compliance with the *Notification of New Substances Regulations 1982** is given in the HSC Approved Code of Practice. Those who have duties under Section 6 may find it useful to refer to this for background information or detailed tests that may be relevant.

*The Notification of New Substances Regulations 1982 SI 1496, as amended by SI 890 1986 and the supporting Approved Code of Practice (currently Annex to Commission Directive 84/449/EC) are intended to ensure that the potential of new chemical substances to cause harm to man or to the natural environment is assessed before they are placed on the European Community market. To achieve this the Regulations require manufacturers and importers intending to place new chemical substances on the market to make known their intentions to do so to the HSE and supply information on the identity and properties of the substances. These notifications are then examined to ensure that the information is adequate for the evaluation of the hazards that may be created by the substance for man and the environment.

The Regulations apply to

"any substance except a substance which had been supplied (either alone or as the component of a preparation) to a person in a Member State at any time in the period from 1 January 1971 to 18 September 1981"

The substances thus excluded are listed in the European Inventory of Existing Commercial Chemical Substances (EINECS).

cont ...

The Regulations do not impose the same notification requirements in respect of all new substances. Some are excluded entirely from the scope of the Regulations; for some others the information which must be submitted is quite limited (for advice see HSE booklet HS(R)14 *A guide to the Notification of New Substances Regulations 1982)*.

Compliance with the notification requirements of the Regulations does not detract from the obligations imposed by Section 6 of the HSW Act on manufacturers or importers, or those imposed under environmental protection law on manufacturers, importers and dischargers.

Labelling

27 The main aims of labelling are:

(a) to identify a particular substance and its container;

(b) to highlight the principal hazards that may arise during the transport, storage and use of the substance;

(c) to set out the basic safety precautions and emergency action to counteract the main known hazards.

Correct labelling can be as important for a consignment of clay or grain as for a drum of chemical.

28 The CPL Regulations and associated Approved List and Approved Code of Practice provide a comprehensive system for classifying and labelling dangerous substances, including mixtures and preparations, which is consistent with most international requirements. These regulations provide for the use of *supply labels* and *conveyance labels* for substances which are subject to them:

The prime function of *supply labels is* to warn/inform the user of both acute and chronic exposure hazards. The label must be on the receptacle from which the dangerous substance is to be dispensed.

The prime function of *conveyance labels is* to warn/inform the transporter, emergency services and the public. Labels must be on those layers of packaging liable to be handled during conveyance (usually the outermost layer). They need only take into account the acute risks posed by the substance.

29 Further advice on the purposes and compilation of labels may be found in the HSE publication HS(R)22 A *guide to the Classification, Packaging and Labelling of Dangerous Substances Regulations 1984.*

30 The statutory CPL label alone would not normally be sufficient to comply with the obligation to provide information under Section 6(4)(c). It would usually need supplementing either by extra information on the container label or by the supply of further written information. The manufacturer should decide what method he needs to use to provide adequate information.

31 Sometimes the information on the container label alone is sufficient to meet the requirement for the provision of information. For example, small packs of substances or preparations such as decorative water-based paints, hand dishwashing products, household cleaners, bleaches and disinfectants used in the janitorial sector may fall into this category. Similar considerations could apply to some agricultural products. In such cases where the product as sold is used or dispensed in containers handled by users, labelling could be the most satisfactory method of communicating information relating to the safe use and hazards of such products.

Product hazard information (data sheets etc)

32 Many forms of information and advice may accompany a substance. Although a model format has not been adopted in the past, there are obvious benefits, especially for the user, in the provision of accurate, comprehensive and consistent information with a uniform layout.

Looking towards the future when the Dangerous Preparations Directive is implemented in 1992, a safety data sheet will be required for mixtures within scope. The content and format of this data sheet is being discussed in the European forum at present.

33 A suggested check list of essential items which need to be considered when preparing any information sheet is given in Appendix 3. The following paragraphs discuss some of these in detail. It must be emphasised that data sheets, for example, should not comprise a simple list of unimaginative script; complying with Section 6 should not be a matter of form filling. Consideration should be given to the content of

the total information package and this will depend on the properties of the substance and the manner in which it is to be used. The package can range from a single page for certain substances of low hazard to extensive booklets of guidance for the use of certain highly hazardous materials, and might usefully include visual aids such as posters, films or pocket-sized cards.

Product name

34 The name of the substance needs to be clear and unambiguous so that the user can easily relate the substance and its container labels with the rest of the information.

Reasonably foreseeable uses

35 Section 6 covers the reasonably foreseeable uses etc of substances. Courts will pay attention to any relevant advice provided to users, for example precautions to be taken or actions to avoid, in deciding whether duties have been complied with. This is also the position under Section 10(2)(a) of Part I of the Consumer Protection Act which also imposes a civil liability about substances used at work. For certain products it may be possible to be quite specific (eg "two pack automotive paint for spray application and oven curing"). However, in many cases a very general description will be all that is possible (eg a drum of toluene could have the general designation "general purpose industrial solvent and a raw material for chemical synthesis").

36 The information should normally be simple and positive, but when it is important for reasons of health and safety that a substance is not used in some specific way, it may be appropriate to include a suitable warning, eg "paint for brush or roller application only - IT MUST NOT BE SPRAYED (consult supplier)".

37 However, when it is reasonably foreseeable that a substance could be put to unintended uses or misused by the user he should give a cautionary warning. For example, organic solvents can also be used for cleansing the hands. This may result in a risk of absorption of the solvent and other contaminants through the skin, or of skin irritation or dermatitis.

Composition

38 Suppliers need to provide relevant and adequate information, but it may not always be necessary, in the interests of health and safety, to disclose full or detailed compositions especially when the components are essentially non-hazardous. Information on the hazardous components of any product or preparation will usually be required by the user so that he may independently assess any residual risks under the specific circumstances of the use of the substance.

39 There may be circumstances when full disclosure of compositions would serve little practical purpose for the user. For example many hydrocarbon solvents are made to a physical specification (eg distillation range) and any one product may contain many individual compounds of concentration varying slightly from batch to batch. Consequently, general, but definitive descriptive terms such as 'White Spirit' or 'Special Boiling Point Solvent No X' may be adequate for the user, provided the major components are identified in accordance with the Classification, Packaging and Labelling of Dangerous Substances Regulations 1984.

40 On the other hand, when a product is supplied as an ingredient for the manufacture of a preparation, full disclosure of the quantity and nature of hazardous constituents in the product may be essential to enable the user to meet his obligations as regards classification and labelling of the manufactured preparation.

41 In some cases the regulations require the actual percentages of toxic and very toxic materials (as defined in the regulations) to be shown on the product label. But even where this is not the case it may be appropriate that it be included in the information package, as well as the names of any harmful or corrosive substances above the stated threshold percentages. The withholding of relevant information on compositions may hinder an employer or other persons who control premises from complying with their duties under Sections 2, 3, 4 and 6 of the HSW Act (see paragraph 2,) and COSHH.

Physical and chemical properties

42 Deciding which properties will be of most relevance in any particular case will depend on the nature of the substance and the reasonably foreseeable uses. A summary of relevant details on physical properties such as boiling point, vapour pressure (at a reference temperature), evaporation rates, vapour density and particle size should be provided. It is particularly helpful if the equilibrium vapour pressure at ambient temperatures and at the likely range of processing temperatures are converted to approximate maximum concentrations in air by volume to enable comparisons to be made with data on fire and health hazards. However, more obvious properties such as slipperiness should not be ignored. Basic information on potentially dangerous reactions with other substances should also be given.

43 Information on properties should be clearly set out, be as brief as possible and be as directly relatable as possible to potential health and safety hazards. Extensive details on chemistry, reaction mechanisms etc, may serve little purpose on a basic data sheet. If such information does have a direct health and safety content rather than a technical or marketing one it may be appropriate to present it in a separate booklet and to refer to it on the basic data sheet.

Health hazards

44 This section should provide information to the user on what is known about potential hazards to health based upon both the results of any relevant tests which have been carried out regarding the toxicity of a substance being supplied and previous experience in its manufacture or use.

45 Even if the results of the relevant tests do not indicate any particular health hazard, no substance should be described as 'safe' or 'non-toxic'.

46 When interpreting the complex results from these tests the advice of qualified toxicologists or medical practitioners may be helpful. The potential routes of exposure to the substance during any reasonably foreseeable conditions of use should be indicated. These may include the inhalation of dust, fume, aerosol or vapour, or ingestion, skin contact or absorption. The likely effects of both short term (acute) and long term (chronic) exposure by the relevant routes should be clearly and briefly summarised, so that any symptoms in the workplace can be quickly recognised. Emphasis should be given to the most significant or any special hazards (eg delayed effects or sensitisation). It should be clearly stated if the toxic effects are due to any particular ingredients.

47 Information on the current exposure limits should be given, and any necessary explanations provided (see current edition of Guidance Note EH 40).

Fire and explosion hazards

48 Information under this heading should include both a description of the inherent hazards of fire or explosion of the substance, and the anticipated consequences if the substance is exposed to fire or excessive heat. In the latter case, the substance itself may not be flammable, but may decompose to give dangerous by-products when heated.

49 Examples of the first element would include such hazard warnings as 'Highly Flammable Liquid', 'Combustible Solid', or 'Containing Flammable Gas'. The second element may include such statements as 'Gives off toxic noxious fumes when heated', or 'Storage temperature must not exceed X°C'. In the case of flammable liquids, a comment on the likelihood of the evolution of heavy flammable vapours and their behaviour would be appropriate.

50 Factual information designed to give assistance towards correct conditions of use, handling, transport, storage and disposal has to be provided (see paragraphs 52 to 59). This information may include the flashpoints for liquids, the minimum ignition temperature for powders and the flammable limits in air or the lower flammable limit as appropriate. (The supplier needs to decide if such information is most effectively given in this section or in the section on properties, paragraphs 42 to 43).

51 All the information provided should be consistent with that required to be given under existing and proposed regulations covering classification, labelling and packaging (see paragraphs 27 to 31). The special problems of

explosive and self-reactive substances including the effects of heat, shock, long term storage etc, should be clearly indicated.

Transport precautions

52 Brief mention should be made of any relevant health and safety legislation (eg the Dangerous Substances (Conveyance by Road in Road Tankers and Tank Containers) Regulations 1981 SI 1059 and the Classification and Labelling of Explosives Regulations 1983 SI 1140). Any special precautions or procedures which a user needs to be aware of or needs to comply with in connection with the transport or conveyance of the substance, either within or outside his premises, should be summarised.

53 When substances are transported on the public highway, information which is required by existing Codes of Practice wil be sufficient in respect of substances subject to the Classification, Packaging and Labelling of Dangerous Substances Regulations 1984, The Road Traffic (Carriage of Dangerous Substances in Packages) Regulations 1986 SI 1951 and the Dangerous Substances (Conveyance by Road in Road Tankers and Tank Containers) Regulations 1981.

Storage precautions

54 General advice should be given on the preferred means of storage to minimise the risks of fire or explosion or the exposure of personnel to health hazards due to spillage, leakage etc. HSE guidance which may be helpful includes CS2 *The storage of highly flammable liquids* and CS17 *Storage of packaged dangerous substances.* Information provided in this section may include:

(a) design of storage rooms, containers, vessels etc;

(b) materials of construction;

(c) storage temperature range;

(d) segregation from incompatible materials;

(e) stability in storage, or potential decomposition reactions.

55 If detailed advice is necessary as, for example, with the design of pressure vessels for the bulk storage of a liquefied gas, it would be appropriate to refer the user to detailed guidance presented in a separate booklet.

Disposal

56 Information has to be given about safe disposal when it is reasonably foreseeable that there may be associated risks to health and safety in that activity, eg in the case of waste lubricating oil, where disposal could involve certain reasonably foreseeable risks, information may be provided on the safest methods of disposal.

Handling, processing and use precautions

57 This is perhaps the key section on which the success or failure of the whole HSW Act Section 6 information package will depend. There are many cases when the manufacturer, importer or supplier will know precisely how a substance will be used because it has been designed to meet a specific purpose or need. In these cases the user should expect precise advice about conditions necessary to ensure that the substance will be safe and without risks to health when it is used. In particular, any appropriate control measures (eg enclosure of plant or equipment, remote handling facilities, local exhaust ventilation) to eliminate or minimise the risks should be clearly outlined.

Personal protection

58 When such control measures need to be supplemented with personal protection, the type of equipment suitable for protection against the residual hazards should be described (eg recommended types and material specification for protective clothing, types of suitable respirators or breathing apparatus).

General use

59 Where a substance is not produced for a specific use or the supplier feels unable to anticipate all the reasonably foreseeable conditions of use (eg with a general-purpose industrial solvent) he should provide general advice on the handling precautions on the basic data sheet and may advise users to consult him for further information. Detailed guidance is probably best given separately rather than in a basic leaflet or data sheet.

Emergency action

60 This section of the information package may be the only opportunity a manufacturer, importer or supplier of a substance will have of ensuring that the information required for prompt and appropriate action to minimise risk in the event of an emergency is provided. Therefore, sound but brief instructions, which may be acted upon in an emergency, are essential. This section should cover the aspects given in the following paragraphs.

The information should include:

Fire

(a) any special hazards arising from combustion and the precautions to be observed;

(b) the correct type of extinguishing agent (and any necessary warnings about the use of certain unsuitable or incompatible extinguishing media);

(c) any special precautions or procedures including advice to be offered to the Fire Brigade.

Spillage

(a) consequences of various foreseeable types of spillage;

(b) precautionary action (including evacuation if appropriate);

(c) procedures to control and treat spillage (including advice on any special protective equipment necessary).

First-aid treatment

Advice should be given on suitable first-aid treatment in the event of 'overexposure' or other potentially hazardous accidental contact with the substance. This should cover incidents arising from hazardous skin or eye contact, ingestion or inhalation of any gas, fume, dust or aerosol in concentrations liable to give rise to acute ill health. The symptoms and effects of such acute exposures may be briefly summarised (see paragraph 46).

Medical information

In those exceptional cases where specific information is necessary for the use of medical practitioners (eg a known specific antidote) this should also be given on the sheet, but kept quite separate from first-aid measures (see paragraph 61). The advice of qualified medical practitioners with knowledge and experience of first-aid in the workplace should be sought to ensure that the guidance is as correct and up-to-date as possible. The HSE's Employment Medical Advisory Service (EMAS) can be consulted.

Emergency contact - telephone number (24 hour service) should also be given if applicable.

Additional information

61 Other information which has not been given elsewhere, but which is relevant to the user, should be listed at the end of the information sheet. The headings may include:

(a) ecological hazards;

(b) relevant legislation;

(c) advice to occupational medical officers;

(d) reference to relevant technical literature, HSE guidance notes, etc.

Part 3 Using the information*

62 In order to make an initial judgement of the adequacy or completeness of the information provided by the manufacturer some employers have found it useful to produce in-house data sheets or hazard information and handling summaries. Any basic omissions can thus be readily identified and the appropriate steps taken, such as further contact with the manufacturer or supplier of the substance. The user's own data sheets can then be used as part, but only part, of what is required when preparing detailed plant operating procedures, operator training programmes etc.

*The advice in this part of the guidance booklet is limited to the principal aspects that need to be considered to ensure the safe use of a substance. The note does not for example include detailed advice on plant design or employee training programmes.

63 For the purposes of COSHH, in particular Regulation 6, a valid and informed assessment needs to be made about the risks to health from hazardous substances used at work. The principle throughout the COSHH Regulations is that the extent of the precautions which should be taken at the workplace are determined by the nature and degree of the risk in the first place. Information which is needed by employers when they make a decision about the degree of hazard from a substance, and their consequent assessment of the nature of downstream controls, comes from several sources. Among these sources are trade and technical literature, HSE guidance notes and data sheets, in-house product and process knowledge from previous experience of use. Information provided by the supplier eg in a safety data sheet, or on a label, however, often plays a key role in the employers' decision making process. Detailed guidance is to be provided under the Regulations about the way in which assessments are to be made.

Specialist assessment

64 Although some of the information provided by the manufacturer may be of a technical nature that needs some specialist judgement the emphasis should be on clear and comprehensive data which requires a minimum of interpretation to be used for effective contact systems. Large companies may have in-house expertise such as toxicologists, medical advisers, occupational hygienists, safety managers, engineers, chemists etc to assist them. A major problem can be the effective coordination of these specialisms in order to make a practical assessment of the information received.

Small firms

65 Most small companies will not have such comprehensive resources and would find it difficult to arrange or finance contact with numerous external experts. In practice the manufacturer, importer or supplier should prepare adequate information under Section 6 which assists the employer to discharge his Section 2 duties. Trade Associations may also provide useful information.

Substance user checklist

66 The preliminary judgement should reveal sufficient information to enable those with responsibilities under the HSW Act Sections 2, 3 and 4, and COSHH, to look in some detail at the safety of the substance in any given situation. The sort of questions that need to be answered include:

(a) is the substance to be accepted for use or should a search for substitutes be pursued?

(b) what type of plant and equipment will allow the substance to be used safely?

(c) is existing plant fully satisfactory or will it need to be modified or replaced?

(d) what additional control measures, such as local exhaust ventilation or personal protective equipment, may be necessary and at which stages of handling, storage or processing would these be applied?

(e) what systems of work will be necessary to eliminate or minimise risk?

(f) what further management and technical controls will be necessary to maintain and to monitor the safety of the operation (eg by atmospheric sampling when employees may be exposed to toxic substances in air)?

(g) what special skills, including the design, commissioning, operation and maintenance of the plant, will be necessary to detail all the necessary arrangements to ensure safe operation?

(h) what information, instruction, training and supervision will be necessary for employees to ensure that the systems of work remain effective?

Information, instruction and training

67 The aim is to ensure that employees, and others at work on the premises, are aware of:

(a) the presence of substances hazardous to health;

(b) the risks from those substances;

(c) the precautions to be observed;

(d) the results of any exposure measurements;

(e) where limits are exceeded, the causes and the measures to be taken to rectify the situation.

68 Information, instruction and training must be adequate to ensure that people understand how to take effective precautions and how to avoid endangering themselves or others. The needs of those who are illiterate or have a poor command of English may call for special attention.

69 Employers and others, such as contractors and emergency services, need to be aware of:

(a) the health, fire or other hazards connected with the substances, where these hazards may be present and how they may be exposed to them;

(b) the reasons for the preventive measures;

(c) the need for the control measures and protective equipment and how, when and where they should be used if they are to be effective (eg the correct way of using respiratory protective equipment);

(d) the significance of environmental monitoring at the workplace, of biological tests and of health surveillance if appropriate;

(e) the need for employees to report defects or inadequacies in the control measures or protective equipment which could affect their health or that of other persons;

(f) the procedure to be followed in an emergency;

(g) the relevant detailed plant operating procedures.

Training methods

70 Information, instruction and training on the use of substances at work should preferably be integrated with and be a normal part of any information, instruction and training given to enable persons to carry out their job function. For example, it may form part of practical training on how to use particular plant or equipment. In some cases, formal training by means of lectures and discussion groups could be appropriate whereas, in other cases, on the job training should be given as appropriate to ensure that the overall objectives are attained. The expertise of safety officers, safety representatives and members of safety committees should also be used when appropriate.

Back-up information

71 As a back-up to such instruction and training, it is desirable that workpeople should have ready access to information relevant to their health and safety at work. For example, reference material may be made available at one or more well-publicised locations or from one or more specified persons (line managers, safety officers, safety representatives etc) on the premises. Material so provided should be checked regularly and kept up to date. Examples of information which may need to be provided in this way would include manufacturers' and suppliers' literature, copies of relevant HSE guidance notes and codes of practice and other authoritative literature including, perhaps, summarised extracts in layman's language of reference sources which may have been consulted (see paragraph 8).

72 Essential information may also be provided in ways other than writing. In particular, audio-visual and graphic/pictorial displays may prove effective.

Placards and posters

73 The prominent display of explanatory placards and posters, which may be published by HSE, some other authoritative body, the supplier or the employer himself, for particular substances or circumstances will play an important part in any scheme for providing information, instruction and training.

Pocket safety cards

74 In some circumstances, however, it may be equally important to issue operators with safety guidance on a personal basis (eg as a pocket-sized card) for ready reference, especially where

their jobs are of a mobile nature or involve the use of substances which have been transferred from their original, labelled containers into smaller ones for more convenient use. Smaller containers must be adequately labelled and not be receptacles that could be mistaken for food or drink containers, for example lemonade bottles.

75 Information about the action necessary in the event of an emergency should be readily available to members of the emergency services at the time of their arrival at the workplace. (See para 60).

Information for the public

76 Finally, it seems appropriate, in the context of providing information on substances used at work to mention the concern which has been expressed by members of the public who have, from time to time, come into contact with chemicals applied to agricultural or amenity land. The extent of such exposure is usually small and may cause no harm, but it can nevertheless be alarming. Anyone affected should at the very least be able to get information as to the identity of the substances concerned to enable him, if he wishes, to seek the reassurance of medical advice. Such information should be readily available from the persons responsible for the application of the chemicals (eg farmer, local authority, contractor etc).

Appendix 1 Health and Safety at Work etc Act 1974 (excerpts)

Section 2 General duties of employers to their employees

General duties

2.-(1) It shall be the duty of every employer to ensure, so far as is reasonably practicable, the health, safety and welfare at work of all his employees.

(2) Without prejudice to the generality of an employer's duty under the preceding subsection, the matters to which that duty extends include in particular -

(a) the provision and maintenance of plant and systems of work that are, so far as is reasonably practicable, safe and without risks to health;

(b) arrangements for ensuring, so far as is reasonably practicable, safety and absence of risks to health in connection with the use, handling, storage and transport of articles and substances;

(c) the provision of such information, instruction, training and supervision as is necessary to ensure, so far as is reasonably practicable, the health and safety at work of his employees;

(d) so far as is reasonably practicable as regards any place of work under the employer's control, the maintenance of it in a condition that is safe and without risks to health and the provision and maintenance of means of access to and egress from it that are safe and without such risk;

(e) the provision and maintenance of a working environment for his employees that is, so far as is reasonably practicable, safe, without risks to health, and adequate as regards facilities and arrangements for their welfare at work.

Section 3 General duties of employers and self-employed to persons other than their employees

3.-(1) It shall be the duty of every employer to conduct his undertaking in such a way as to ensure, so far as is reasonably practicable, that persons not in his employment who may be affected thereby are not thereby exposed to risks to their health or safety.

(2) It shall be the duty of every self-employed person to conduct his undertaking in such a way as to ensure, so far as is reasonably practicable, that he and other persons (not being his employees) who may be affected thereby are not thereby exposed to risks to their health or safety.

Section 6 General duties of manufacturers etc as regards articles and substances for use at work

6-(4) It shall be the duty of any person who manufactures, imports or supplies any substance -

(a) to ensure, so far as is reasonably practicable, that the substance will be safe and without risks to health at all times when it is being used, handled, processed, stored, or transported by a person at work or in premises to which section 4 above applies;

(b) to carry out or arrange for the carrying out of such testing and examination as may be necessary for the performance of the duty imposed on him by the preceding paragraph;

(c) to take such steps as are necessary to secure that persons supplied by that person with the substance are provided with adequate information about any risks to health or safety to which the inherent properties of the substance may give rise, about the results of any relevant tests which have been carried out on or in connection with the substance and about any conditions necessary to ensure that the substance will be safe and without risks to health at all such times as are mentioned in paragraph (a) above and when the substance is being disposed of; and

(d) to take such steps as are necessary to secure, so far as is reasonably practicable, that persons so supplied are provided with all such revisions of information provided to them by virtue of the preceding paragraph as are necessary by reason of its becoming known that anything gives rise to a serious risk to health or safety.

(5) It shall be the duty of any person who undertakes the manufacture of any substance to carry out or arrange for the carrying out of any necessary research with a view to the discovery and, so far as is reasonably practicable, the elimination or minimisation of any risks to health or safety to which the substance may give rise at all such times as are mentioned in paragraph (a) of subsection (4) above.

(6) Nothing in the preceding provisions of this section shall be taken to require a person to repeat any testing, examination or research which has been carried out otherwise than by him or at his instance, in so far as it is reasonable for him to rely on the results thereof for the purposes of those provisions.

Section 7 General duties of employees at work

It shall be the duty of every employee while at work -

(a) to take reasonable care for the health and safety of himself and of other persons who may be affected by his acts or omissions at work; and

(b) as regards any duty or requirement imposed on his employer or any other person by or under any of the relevant statutory provisions, to co-operate with him so far as is necessary to enable that duty or requirement to be performed or complied with.

Appendix 2 Section 6 amendments in force 1 March 1988

Before 1 March	*After 1 March*
Section 6(4) **What is the duty of Importers?**	Original Section 6(7) unchanged, but now qualified by an additional subsection under paragraph 8. After the said subsection (8) there shall be inserted the following subsection - *"8(A) Nothing in subsection (7) or (8) above shall relieve any person who imports any article or substance from any duty in respect of anything which -* *(a) in the case of an article designed outside the United Kingdom, was done by and in the course of any trade, profession or other undertaking carried on by, or was within the control of, the person who designed the article; or* *(b) in the case of an article or substance manufactured outside the United Kingdom,*

was done by and in the course of any trade, profession or other undertaking carried on by, or was within the control of, the person who manufactured the article or substance."

Before 1 March	After 1 March
(i) Importers duty is restricted to matters within their control. (6(7))	(i) Importers duty widened to parallel that of domestic manufacturers. The intention is that imported goods should not be subject to any less stringent safety provisions than domestically produced ones. Nor should foreign manufacturers be allowed to gain competitive advantages in terms of cost savings by not carrying out relevant tests or providing adequate information. If an importer can be shown to be importing products which are not 'safe and without risks to health', the onus is on him to ensure so far as is reasonably practicable that the foreign manufacturer rectifies these, or failing this he should no longer import the products in question.

What does the duty extend to?

Before 1 March	After 1 March
(ii) Substance restricted by 'for use at work'.	(ii) Restriction removed: the duty covers all substances. Substances may have many end uses for work and domestic situations, but there will almost invariably be an at-work application so there is no need to specify this.

Section 6(4)(a) **What is the duty?**

Before 1 March	After 1 March
"To ensure, so far as is reasonably practicable, that the substance is safe and without risks to health when properly *(i)* used *(ii)":*	*"To ensure so far as is reasonably practicable, that the substance will be safe and without risks to health* at all times when it is being used, handled, processed, stored or transported *by a person at work or in* premises *to which* Section 4 applies;"
	Three changes
(i) Limitation to proper use.	(i) Qualifications of 'proper' removed. Manufacturers could previously issue instructions about 'proper use' which ignored uses it was reasonable to suppose would occur in practice. (Sec 6(10)).
(ii) 'Use' is not defined.	(ii) 'Use' is extended: handled, processed, stored or transported are now included. The original definition was too narrow. The duty extends to each and every occasion of use 'at all times'.

Before 1 March	After 1 March
	(iii) Section 4 is specifically mentioned with regard to premises other than work premises. This section places duties on persons who control premises which are non-domestic and used as a place of work where substances are made available, eg launderettes.
Section 6(4)(b) **How is the duty discharged?**	
(a) *By testing*	
"To carry out or arrange for the carrying out of such testing and examination as may be necessary for the performance of the duty imposed on him by the preceding paragraph:"	*"To carry out or arrange for the carrying out of such testing and examination as may be necessary for the performance of the duty imposed on him by the preceding paragraph:"*
Testing is limited to the substance being safe and without risk to health while being 'properly used'.	The tests have to cover the extended range of uses covered by the duty.
Section 6(4)(c)	
(b) *By the communication of information*	
"To take such steps as are necessary to secure that there will be available (i) *in connection with the* use (ii) *of the* substance (iii) at work *adequate information about the results of any relevant tests which have been carried out on or in connection with the substance and about any conditions necessary to ensure that it will be safe and without risks to health* when properly used (iv)*."*	*"To take such steps as are necessary to secure that persons supplied by that person with the substance are provided with adequate information about any risks to health or safety to which the inherent properties of the substance may give rise, about the results of any relevant tests which have been carried out on or in connection with the substance and about any conditions necessary to ensure that the substance will be safe and without risks to health at all such times as are mentioned in paragraph 6(4)(a) above and when the substance is being disposed of; and ..."*
(i) *Limited* to: 'make available' information.	(i) Now has a positive duty to provide adequate information.
(ii) Substance for 'use' *no* extended definition.	(ii) Information has to cover range of activities in 6(4)(a) and disposal.
(iii) Applies to 'at work' only.	(iii) 'Work' restriction removed from substances but Section 6 only applies to work activities and Section 4 premises.
(iv) Proper use only.	(iv) Limitation of 'proper use' removed. The test now is reasonably foreseeable uses.

Before 1 March	*After 1 March*
What provision is there for updating information?	New Section 6(4)
No specific requirement for information to be updated.	A new requirement: *"to take such steps as are necessary to secure, so far as is reasonably practicable that persons so supplied (with substances) are provided with all such revisions of information provided to them by reason of its becoming known that anything gives rise to a serious risk of health and safety".* Information has to be up to date with the state of the art. If a serious risk such as a carcinogenic property becomes evident from use, experience or other data, this has to be communicated to past customers. This duty is limited by so far as is reasonably practicable - the cost and difficulty of locating past customers may be taken into account.
"It shall be the duty of any person who undertakes the manufacture of any substance for use at work to carry out or arrange for the carrying out of any necessary research with a view to the discovery and, so far as is reasonably practicable, the elimination or minimisation of any risks to health or safety to which the substance may give rise."	Limitation of substance for use at work removed. Duty extended to cover all uses ie storage, handling etc.
Section 6(6) **Repetition of tests - what is needed?**	
"Nothing in the preceding provisions of this section shall be taken to require a person to repeat any testing, examination or research which has been carried out otherwise than by him or at his instance, in so far as it is reasonable for him to rely on the results thereof for the purposes of those provisions."	No change No need to repeat tests if it is reasonable to rely on the results of tests carried out by others.
Section 6(7) **Duty - does it extend beyond trade/business activities?**	
"Any duty imposed on any person by any of the preceding provisions of this section shall extend only to things done in the course of a trade, business or other undertaking carried on by him (whether for profit or not) and to matters within his control." Duty restricted in scope to these activities	No change - duty restricted to trade, business etc.

Before 1 March	*After 1 March*
Section 6(10) **What defences are there for the supplier?**	
The duty to make available information is restricted to *proper use*.	The *qualification of 'proper' use is replaced by reasonable foreseeability.*
As a defence an article or substance was not to be regarded as *properly used* where it was used without regard to any relevant information or advice relating to its use which has been made available by a person by whom it was designed, manufactured, imported or supplied.	For subsection (10) (meaning of 'properly used') there shall be substituted the following subsection -
	"(10) For the purposes of this section an absence of safety or a risk to health shall be disregarded in so far as the case in or in relation to which it would arise is shown to be one the occurrence of which could not reasonably be foreseen; *and in determining whether any duty imposed by virtue of paragraph ...6(4) above has been performed regard shall be had to any relevant information or advice which has been provided to any person by the person by whom the substance has been manufactured, imported or supplied."*
	So the qualification that a substance is not regarded as being properly used unless it is used in accordance with the information or advice given by the manufacturer etc is removed. It is replaced by the need for them to consider reasonable foreseeability in their estimate of risk to health and safety. Only in cases where an absence of safety or risk to health could not be reasonably foreseen can they discharge their duty. Previously manufacturers etc could issue instructions about proper use which ignored uses it was reasonable to suppose would occur in practice. Courts interpreted the Section to exclude foreseeable operator error. The intention is to restrict the bounds of the requirement to reasonably foreseeable uses, not to a whole range of uses some of which could be bizarre or unreasonable. Courts will take into account the information (and warnings) in deciding whether the duty under 6(4) has been met.

Appendix 3: Check list

PRODUCT NAME

USES

COMPOSITION

PHYSICAL AND CHEMICAL PROPERTIES

HEALTH HAZARDS

FIRE HAZARDS

STORAGE PRECAUTIONS

TRANSPORT PRECAUTIONS

HANDLING/USE PRECAUTIONS
(including advice on personal protective equipment)

DISPOSAL PRECAUTIONS

EMERGENCY ACTION
Fire, spillage, first aid

ADDITIONAL INFORMATION
Ecological hazards
Relevant regulations
Advice to Occupational Medical Officers
References

NAME, ADDRESS AND TELEPHONE NUMBER OF SUPPLIER

REFERENCE NUMBER, DATE OF ISSUE

Appendix 4 Questions and answers about the new requirements of Section 6 that came into force on 1 March 1988, concerning substances

Introduction

This Appendix sets out in a simple question and answer form some responses to common queries which have been raised by industry about the scope and nature of the 1988 amendments to Section 6. The Appendix has already been issued as an informal guidance note to assist manufacturers, suppliers etc while the revision to HS(G)27 was being prepared.

Question 1 What does Section 6 do?

Answer It requires people who manufacture, import or supply substances to consider and to take reasonably practicable steps to minimise or eliminate the danger from substances when they are used. It also requires them to provide adequate information about the substance when it is supplied to the user.

Question 2 Who has the duty to comply with the requirements of Section 6 about substances?

Answer Manufacturers, importers and suppliers of substances. This includes wholesale distributors, agents and everyone in the supply chain.

Question 3 Do the requirements of Section 6 apply to all substances?

Answer Yes. The manufacturer, supplier or importer of substances must ensure, so far as is reasonably practicable, that all substances should be safe and without risk to health. It is necessary to take into account the seriousness of the risk from the substance when considering what has to be done to discharge the duty in a reasonably practicable way under this Section. If a careful assessment of the risk shows it to be comparatively small and unimportant, the action needed is less than if it is high. The emphasis is on careful assessment of the inherent hazard of the substance to establish reasonably foreseeable risk to health and safety. A supplier of purified water would still have duties under the Section, but the scale of testing needed and information provided would be substantially less than that of a supplier of concentrated sulphuric acid.

Question 4 What activities is Section 6 intended to cover?

Answer The use, handling, storage or transportation of substances by a person at work or in premises to which Section 4 applies. In the case of information it also covers disposal.

Question 5 In view of the apparent application of S6 to all substances does it therefore apply to consumer products for exclusive use in the home?

Answer No, there is separate legislation relating to consumer safety (the other parts of the Consumer Protection Act for example). However certain people who *work* in domestic premises (eg painters and decorators) may use substances and these are subject to this section of the act.

Question 6 What is a 'substance'?

Answer 'Substance' is defined under Section 53 of the Health and Safety at Work etc. Act 1974 as meaning any natural or artificial substance, whether in solid or liquid form, or in the form of a gas or vapour. Micro-organisms are included in the definition and are defined as any microscopic biological entity which is capable of replication. Among the common terms used to describe substances are materials, chemicals, mixtures and preparations. Many are of a complex composition such as paints, solvents or cleaning fluids.

Question 7 What do the manufacturers, importers, etc need to do to comply with their duty?

Answer First of all they must consider the significant characteristic properties of the substance which is intended for supply to the user. What reasonably foreseeable dangers does it give rise to in its reasonably foreseeable uses, either for example as a health hazard, or as an explosive or fire risk from its physical properties? Often these considerations would precede the development of a new project.

Question 8 How can a manufacturer find out about these properties?

Answer Existing information about a substance from technical reference sources, Trade Associations etc, can be used if it is reasonable to rely on the results of this existing research. Thought should be given as to whether it is up to date and relevant. Account must also be taken of any information which is used to classify and label the substance for the purpose of the CPL Regulations.

Question 9 What if there is no such information available?

Answer It will be necessary to carry out or arrange for relevant tests to be carried out. The object will be to find out what hazards, both in terms of health and physico-chemical properties, the substance presents, with a view to the discovery and, so far as is reasonably practicable, the elimination or minimisation of any risk to health and safety to which the substance gives rise. Sometimes it is possible for a substance to be made less hazardous by the elimination of an impurity in the mixture, or the addition of a stabiliser. On occasions the reduction of the danger may be achieved by the packaging used or by distributing it in small quantities. Addition of stenching agents to gases is another example of hazard reduction. It may be discovered that one substance is so hazardous that it is necessary to substitute a less hazardous substance which is equally effective for the same purpose. A manufacturer may have the facilities to do the necessary testing, but there are test-houses who will do the work.

Question 10 But the fact remains that a large number of substances have properties which are inherently hazardous and can cause risks to health and safety which cannot be eliminated. What should be done then?

Answer Substances are different from articles. Many are inherently dangerous and are intended for inherently dangerous uses, so the basic requirement to ensure, so far as is reasonably practicable, that substances will be safe and without risk to health is of limited effect in isolation. It is also necessary to ensure that those at risk are made fully aware of the hazards so that they can take the necessary precautions and control measures. The manufacturer knows about the hazards from the details of the tests carried out on the substance, for example the toxicity rating from the LD_{50} value, or the level of the flammability from the physico-chemical tests.

Question 11 How do manufacturers pass on this information?

Answer They must take such steps as are necessary to ensure that persons supplied with a substance or substances are *provided* with *adequate* information about the hazards of the inherent properties which may give rise to risks to health and safety in use, about the results of any relevant tests, and any conditions necessary to ensure that the substance is safe and without risks to health when being used, handled, processed, stored or transported or being disposed of.

Question 12 What does 'provide' mean?

Answer It requires a positive action to give information to the user. Manufacturers have to make sure that when they supply a substance to a third party, at the time of supply the customer is also given adequate information, usually in the form of a data sheet. Information need not be given for each and every act of supply of the identical substance, probably for regular customers yearly or even longer intervals might be sufficient. If the substance is sold to a third party who is a distributor who then supplies to someone else, the distributor then has the duty of passing on the information as the link in the supply chain. If the distributor modifies a substance, then it is necessary to consider what further adequate 'information' needs to be provided; similar considerations will apply to a user who carries out research and development work on a substance and then re-sells it.

Question 13 Is using the label enough to 'provide' information?

Answer Not usually. The label is often too small an area to do this effectively. But having said this, there are circumstances where for substances of limited hazard the label may be a sufficient source of information. Manufacturers have to decide whether the amount of information they can put on a label is adequate. The user is likely to read and understand a clear and uncluttered label.

Question 14 What is 'adequate'?

Answer Many substances have a multitude of uses and the information must cover any reasonably foreseeable risks to health and safety to which their inherent properties may give rise. It includes the results and interpretations of any relevant tests which have been carried out on or in connection with the substance, and information about the conditions necessary to ensure that the substance will be safe and without risk to health when it is used. (See Answer 9). A manufacturer may know that a particular customer is using a substance for a specific purpose, for example in a laboratory. In such cases the information, as well as giving the broad spectrum of uses, should be tailored for the customer's specific needs. A dialogue can often usefully be established between the customer and the supplier in cases where a more specific approach is helpful. The manufacturer may also need to specify in some detail the conditions necessary in the use of the substances. If a substance must not be used in a specific way it is appropriate to provide suitable warning, "paint for brush or roller application only, must not be sprayed" or, "use only in a closed system".

Question 15 What if a new serious risk to health and safety from the substance comes to light after it has been supplied?

Answer A new requirement has been introduced to make sure that information provided to users takes account of advances in technical knowledge or user experience which reveal previously unknown significant hazards. So the manufacturer has to take reasonably practicable steps to secure that people supplied with the substance are provided with the revised information. One way of alerting past customers who may be difficult to trace may be to put some detail in relevant Trade Journals.

Question 16 Can I discharge my duty if I obtain a written undertaking from the user to relieve me of my duty?

Answer No, that option is only given to manufacturers of articles. It is intended, among other things, for manufacturers of, for example, components or prototypes which are to be further developed by the customer. Substances, even if only supplied in pilot quantities, have inherent properties which may or may not be hazardous, but need to be considered in information to be provided to the user.

Question 17 Importers may have to rely on what the manufacturer outside the United Kingdom sends them in the way of information. Can they limit their duty to take this into account?

Answer No, their duty is the same as that of UK manufacturers or suppliers. If they find that the person who supplies them does not allow them to comply with the requirements of Section 6 (eg fails to provide them with adequate information), they will have to stop supplying the substance or themselves take steps to ensure compliance. The intention is that imported goods should not be subject to any less stringent safety provisions than domestically produced ones. Foreign manufacturers should not be able to gain a competitive advantage in terms of cost savings by not eliminating or minimising risks to health and safety or by not providing adequate information. If importers receive information in a foreign language, then it must be translated into English for supply on the UK market. Importers must satisfy themselves that the information they provide is adequate.

Question 18 If a substance is supplied under a credit sale agreement, conditional sale agreement, etc, is the person who does the financing responsible for discharging the duties under this Section?

Answer No, the 'supplier' is still regarded as the manufacturer etc for the purposes of discharging the duty.

Question 19 Can suppliers use the fact that they have provided adequate information for reasonably foreseeable uses as evidence that they have discharged their legal duty?

Answer Yes, the assessment of risk is confined to the 'reasonably foreseeable' uses which restrict the bounds of the duty to exclude bizarre uses. So if there is an occurrence or accident arising from the use of a substance which causes risks to health and safety, the duty to consider those risks only applies if they could have been reasonably foreseen. It is necessary however to consider the effects and risks when a substance is being used in any process which the supplier is actually aware that the customer is carrying out.

Question 20 Is there a prescribed format for the information which has to be provided?

Answer No, useful detail is given in the guidance supplied by the HSE and the checklist (Appendix 3) gives an outline of the points to consider. Information about the risks to health and safety for the range of activities in Question 11 should be given. Risks from storage or transport may be different to those when the substance is being processed or handled.

Question 21 What information is needed for transport?

Answer For the transport of substances on the public highway, information which is required by existing Codes of Regulations is sufficient in respect of substances subject to those Regulations (Classification, Packaging and Labelling of Dangerous Substances Regulations 1984; Road Traffic (Carriage of Dangerous Substances in Packages etc) Regulations 1986; Dangerous Substances (Conveyance by Road in Road Tankers and Tank Containers) Regulations 1981). When substances are delivered to a site manufacturers have to provide the user with enough information to discharge their Section 2, 3 or 4 duties, and their duties as consignor if they re-supply the substance for conveyance to other destinations either in the UK or abroad. For substances which are not covered by these Regulations, any special precautions or procedures which are needed for their safe transport should be given.

Question 22 Does a manufacturer need to disclose the full composition of the substance in the information which is provided?

Answer Each case needs to be considered separately. It may not be necessary in the interests of health and safety to disclose full compositions especially when the components are essentially non-hazardous; but the witholding of relevant information on compositions may hinder employers from complying with their duties under Sections 2 and 3 of HSWA. It may also make it impossible for them to comply with the requirements of the CPL Regulations about the classification of substances and preparations. There is, too, the assessment under the COSHH Regulations to be considered.

Appendix 5 HSE Area Offices

Area Offices normally operate between 8.30-17.00 Monday to Friday. The police have names and telephone numbers of local HSE staff who may be contacted in the event of an emergency outside office hours.

Area		*Address*	*Telephone Number*
1	**South West**	Inter City House, Mitchell Lane, Victoria Street, Bristol BS1 6AN	0272 290681
2	**South**	Priestley House, Priestley Road Basingstoke RG24 9NW	0256 473181
3	**South East**	3 East Grinstead House, London Road, East Grinstead, West Sussex RH19 1RR	0342 326922
5	**London N**	Maritime House, 1 Linton Road, Barking, Essex 1G11 8HF	081-594 5522
6	**London S**	1 Long Lane, London SE1 4PG	071-407 8911
7	**East Anglia**	39 Baddow Road, Chelmsford, Essex CM2 OHL	0245 284661
8	**Northern Home Counties**	14 Cardiff Road, Luton, Beds LU1 1PP	0582 34121
9	**East Midlands**	Belgrave House, 1 Greyfriars, Northampton NN1 2BS	0604 21233
10	**West Midlands**	McLaren Bldg, 2 Masshouse Circus, Queensway, Birmingham B4 7NP	021-200 2299
11	**Wales**	Brunel House, 2 Fitzalan Road, Cardiff CF2 1SH	0222 473777
12	**Marches**	The Marches House, Midway, Newcastle-under-Lyme, Staffs ST5 1DT	0782 717181
13	**North Midlands**	Birkbeck House, Trinity Square, Nottingham NG1 4AU	0602 470712
14	**South Yorkshire**	Sovereign House, 40 Silver Street, Sheffield S1 2ES	0742 739081
15	**W & N Yorks**	8 St Pauls Street, Leeds LS1 2LE	0532 446191
16	**Greater Manchester**	Quay House, Quay Street, Manchester M3 3JB	061-831 7111
17	**Merseyside**	The Triad, Stanley Road, Bootle L20 3PG	051-922 7211
18	**North West**	Victoria House, Ormskirk Road, Preston, PR1 1HH	0772 59321
19	**North East**	Arden House, Regent Centre, Gosforth, Newcastle-upon-Tyne, NE3 3JM	091-284 8448
20	**Scotland East**	Belford House, 59 Belford Road, Edinburgh EH4 3UE	031-225 1313
21	**Scotland West**	314 St Vincent Street, Glasgow G3 8XG	041-204 2646